Taking The "Duh" Out Of
DIVORCE

Written & Illustrated by
Trevor Romain

©2009 The Trevor Romain Company, Austin, TX

©The Trevor Romain Company
www.TrevorRomain.com

Dedication

For all of my little friends at the Botshabelo Orphanage in Magaliesburg, South Africa.

Table of Contents

Introduction

The word divorce means the end of a marriage.
Parents who get divorced sign special papers that
say the marriage is legally over.

Divorce can make even the smartest person in
the world say, "Duh, I don't know what to do or
how to feel."

A number of years ago I got divorced. At the
time I thought it was the worst thing that could
ever happen to anyone. I was sad, embarrassed and
I couldn't sleep. My stomach hurt. I even threw up
a few times.

When people get divorced they often have a really hard time. So do their kids.

Divorce is an uncomfortable experience for the whole family. Nobody likes it, not even the mom or dad who decided to end the marriage.

During my visits to schools across the country, I have spoken to many young people whose parents have split up. Most of these kids couldn't find answers to the million questions they had about the divorce.

If your parents are getting divorced and you're trying to make sense of it all, I wrote this book for you. I know you are having a hard time trying to understand what's going on, no matter how brave and strong you are. I hope I can answer some of the difficult questions you might have about what you are experiencing. I hope this book gives you the words and strength you need during this tough time. I hope it helps you take the "duh" out of your parents' divorce.

And I hope you believe me when I say that you won't always feel as sad, confused, and upset as you are possibly feeling right now.

1
Why do parents get divorced?

As people grow, they change. It's a natural part of life. The same thing happens with some marriages. Moms and dads change as they grow and sometimes the change doesn't suit one or both of the partners in the marriage. Actually, the same thing happens in many friendships—and you might have already experienced it.

It happened to me. I made a friend in kindergarten. We were best friends until fourth grade. Then we both started liking different things and hanging out with different people. By sixth grade we had both changed so much that we had nothing in common anymore and our friendship ended. (When he started putting sugar on his eggs and syrup on his burgers, I knew it was over!) Should we have stayed friends because we used to like each other? I don't think so.

After being married for a while, some moms and dads grow even closer while others grow further apart. They stop caring. They don't listen to one another anymore. They yell and fight. They're frustrated and unhappy.

Should they stay together just because they used to be in love? Probably not.

Some parents who grow apart stay married because they don't want to upset their children. Check this out: experts say that children living with unhappily married parents are often more stressed and less happy than children whose parents are successfully divorced.

Yikes! This divorce thing is not easy! Parents freak out. Kids feel awful. Grandparents don't know what to do. Friends don't know whose side to take. It's hard. But believe me, it doesn't stay messy forever, and often the divorce turns out to be the best thing for the families who go through it.

2
If splitting up is so hard,
then why are they doing it?

Divorce is probably one of the hardest things your parents will face in their lives. This might seem confusing to you because, hello, they are the ones who decided to get divorced. So, why are they doing it?

They are doing it because they know that unhappy parents create unhappy homes. They're doing it because they believe the family has a better chance of happiness if the two of them live apart. They're doing it because no matter how hard they tried to make the marriage work, they just don't feel they can.

It's a tough decision. Your parents probably know that you want them to stay together, and they might feel terribly guilty about it, but feeling guilty is no reason to stay married. And they honestly believe that getting divorced is the best option.

3
Do I have a say in any of this?

This is going to sound really awful, but there isn't much you can do to stop your parents from getting a divorce.

Children involved in divorce often try to get their parents to love each other again. But the truth is, nobody can make anybody love anybody else. Your parents have made a choice, and it's something you will not be able to change no matter how hard you try.

Many children who are going through a divorce dream that their parents will get back together, but that very seldom happens.

Your parents have made what they believe is the best choice, and by the time they tell you their decision, they've thought about it a lot and have pretty much made up their minds.

Rather than putting your energy into trying to get your parents to stay together, put your energy into helping yourself stay strong.

4

Do you think my parents still love me?

In the dictionary, divorce is described as a legal judgment that ends a marriage. It does not say, "Divorce is when parents stop loving their children and go off and find a couple of new kids to take their place. Especially kids who keep their rooms clean and love broccoli."

Your parents were in love when they got married. You were born out of that love. Divorce happens because parents stop loving each other, not because they stop loving you!

Other than wanting to throw up when they hear that their parents are splitting up, many kids automatically think they won't be loved anymore. This is not the case. Your parents love you and need your love as they go through one of the toughest things they will likely ever face.

Your parents will probably be more stressed than usual, and they might be too distracted to reassure you as much as you need. If you're unsure about their love, the best thing is to tell them how you feel.

5
Can I ask my parents questions about their divorce?

Absolutely. If you have unanswered questions, you will probably worry and feel quite lonely. Your parents don't want you to feel this way and will most likely be happy to answer your questions.

Parents usually don't say much about the divorce because they are trying to protect you and they don't want to upset you. They might be feeling emotional and may find it hard to talk about the divorce. And there are some things they will want to keep private. But you should be able to ask them questions about the things that affect you, like, "When are you getting divorced?", "Who will take care of me?", "Do we have to move?", and "Do you still love me?"

If you find it hard to ask questions face-to-face but you really need answers, send your parents an e-mail or a letter.

6

This might sound crazy, but is it okay to help my parents?

Moms and dads can get really angry with each other during a divorce. It's pretty normal for them to argue, and it's pretty normal for you to want to stop them. It's important to remember that you cannot work things out for them. They need to do it for themselves. Your job is to stay calm. And, as you already know, it's not always easy!

Normally, your parents are there to help you, but during a divorce they might be stressed, angry, distracted, sad, confused, depressed, or all of the above. And they might need your help. It's perfectly fine to try to help them get through this difficult time. Although you can't make them feel better and you might be feeling pretty bad yourself, you can try to be sympathetic. It will be easier for everyone if you all remember to be understanding and kind to each other.

A good way to help your parents is to be honest about how you are feeling and let them know in a calm way what you need. If they know this, they can help you feel safe and loved.

7

I'm freaking out because I think I caused my parents to split up.

Don't freak out! Take a chill pill and listen to this: Never in the history of the world has a child ever actually caused a divorce. (They have caused a lot of other things—like the invention of the scooter, and major stress on Santa Claus—but not divorce.)

If you think the divorce happened because of something you did or didn't do, think again. Your behavior or attitude has nothing to do with your parents' divorce. (If you've been a pain in the neck, you might have driven your parents crazy, but they didn't split up because you didn't do your chores!)

I hope it's not my fault that my parents are splitting up.

This is the situation. Your parents decided to split up because of their relationship with each other, not because of their relationship with you.

If a parent seems inattentive, mean, or uncaring, you might feel they're blaming you for the split. As you know by now (because I keep repeating it), divorce is not easy for anyone in the family. Moms and dads going through a breakup are often extremely stressed, and stress can cause them to act differently and sometimes rather strangely. Try not to take it personally.

Warning! You know how sometimes you say things you don't mean in the heat of the moment? How during a fight you might blurt out that you hate someone without really meaning it? Sometimes parents say things they don't mean while they are going through a divorce. During one of these bad moments, they might say something very hurtful. If this happens, don't believe it. Wait until everyone is calm and ask about it.

8
What's up with this silly pain that won't go away?

The pain from a divorce is not like the pain you get from hitting your thumb with a hammer. The pain from a sore thumb can be treated with ice, some medicine, and a huge bandage.

The pain from a divorce can't be treated with a bandage or ice, but it can be eased a lot by talking. Believe it or not, keeping your feelings to yourself makes the pain harder to take, and talking about it makes it easier to deal with.

You can talk to friends, family members, school counselors, priests or rabbis, and even your parents. Your mom and dad might be so busy with their own pain that they forget to ask you about yours. An honest, open talk can make you feel closer—and be helpful for all of you.

Even if you have many people to talk to, you might want to speak to someone who has experience in helping kids through divorce. Ask your parents to arrange for an appointment with a counselor. Counselors know exactly what you are going through, and they can give you the tools you need to deal with your pain.

9
Is it okay to cry?

Divorce is often compared to death because the grief is similar to what one feels when someone has died. Crying, as you know, is a natural way to deal with death and loss. And divorce—the ending of your family as you know it—is a huge loss.

If you think crying isn't cool, think again. Crying helps you express your emotions and acts as a release valve to let go of the awful sadness and pain that builds up inside you. You will almost always feel better after you have cried.

Most people prefer to be alone when they cry because they feel embarrassed, but don't be ashamed to cry in front of people. It's a great way to let them know you need support.

10
Will I ever feel better?

You will feel better, I promise. It might not happen tomorrow or next week or even next month, but eventually you will become comfortable with your new life as a person with divorced parents.

Going through a divorce is like experiencing a tornado in your backyard. First you notice black clouds slowly building up on the horizon. The sky gets darker and darker as the storm develops.

Then comes the rain and howling wind. You hold on for dear life as the tornado touches down in your yard and tries to rip your home from around you. You're frightened, and you feel like the whole world is coming apart.

Then guess what? It slowly moves off into the distance and later, as the clouds disappear, the sun shines again. No matter how bad the storm is, the sun always shines after it's gone. The same will happen to you during and after a divorce. Just find a safe place and hang on until it's over.

Then pull back the shades in your mind and let the sun stream back into your life.

11
I think I'll explode soon if I don't get rid of my anger.

Let's face it. It's not easy to be calm and sweet when your whole darn world is turning upside down and inside out and you believe your parents are messing up your life.

You might be so angry you want to scream and shout and smash things to pieces. It's okay to be angry. In fact, it's fine to be angry. You just have to find the right way to deal with this very powerful emotion.

Your anger needs to come out or it will chew up your insides and make you feel terrible. I've said this before: talking is one of the best ways to feel better. But if no one is around and you feel as if you're going to explode, use these tried-and-true Anger Busters. You'll feel a whole lot better (and there'll be a lot less to clean up)!

* Squeeze marshmallows until they ooze through your fingers.

* Turn your pillow into a wrestling opponent.

* Scream into your pillow.

* Jump up and down until you're exhausted.

* Create a frustration journal. Write about how you feel.

* Go for a jog and stomp the ground with every step.

* Walk your dog, kick a ball, shoot hoops, sing at the top of your voice.

* Get to know what makes you feel better—and do it!

Warning! People often take their anger out on other people, especially those closest to them. This will not make you feel better. Share your frustration with people you care about instead of using it against them.

12

What if I just want to be left alone?

Being alone can sometimes be exactly what the doctor ordered.

Having a little time to yourself to try to work out what's happening and to understand what you're feeling is fine, but cutting yourself off from the world too much will make you feel even worse.

If you don't want to be with people at all and you feel like you need to hide out, this is when you really need help. Please ask for it. As I said before, talk to your friends, family members, school counselors, priests or rabbis, and even your parents.

13

I'm worried about what my friends will think.

It's completely normal to feel awkward when your parents split up, especially when it comes to your friends. Most people worry about how their friends will react to the news.

It's really important to let your friends know what's going on. More often than not they'll be understanding and supportive, whereas hiding the truth from them will only make you feel worse. It might be easier to tell one friend at a time. Start with your best friend, then he or she can help you tell your other friends.

More than a million kids in this country alone experience divorce every year, so there are a lot of kids who know exactly what you're going through. Maybe you even know some yourself. If so, talk to them about what helped them get through the breakup.

14
Is it okay to still laugh and have fun?

Of course it is! Divorce is not the end of your life, it's just the beginning of a new and different chapter. Laughter and fun are great stress relievers, and having fun with your friends can actually help you deal with what's going on.

Don't feel guilty if you are having a good time even when your parents are not. Being miserable will not make it any easier for you or for them. And there will be times when they can relax and laugh, too.

15
I feel as if I'm being pulled apart!

You love your mom. You love your dad. They don't love each other. They both love you! Wow. What a mess.

Moms and dads can get really angry with each other during a divorce. They might say mean things to each other. They might say mean things about each other. One of them might even use guilt and threats to force you to take sides, and you might feel as if you're being pulled in two different directions at one time. If one of your parents is trying to make you dislike the other, or is making you feel as if you have to choose between them, then they're not being cool. And they're not being fair.

Getting a divorce does not give any parent the right to make their children choose one parent over the other.

YOU DO NOT HAVE TO CHOOSE! It is
okay to love both parents equally, now and forever,
no matter what they say about each other and no
matter who's to blame for the divorce. It's okay to
say, "I love you both and I'm not taking sides."

16

Can one parent actually handle the "zoo" we call our home?

It is going to be hard for both of your parents to start new homes, especially if there are a bunch of wild and crazy children using their homes as jumping castles. Understanding that it's tough for everyone will make the transition into your new living situation a lot easier. But having a happy home is good for everybody, including you, so it's worth putting some effort into making it happen.

Remember, your parents might not be feeling or acting like they normally do. You can really make a difference by helping out and taking care of some of the chores. This might be hard to do, especially if you're feeling angry and hurt. But helping out and working as a team will not only make things easier all around, it will help you feel closer to your parents.

My advice: Don't wait for your parents to ask for your help. You can make a huge difference by stepping up. (Doing this might even help you feel more in control, and that's a good thing.)

17

How am I supposed to live in two homes at one time?

Boy. Having two messy rooms instead of one. Hmmm. That could be interesting. I bet you have a hard time finding stuff in one room, let alone two.

Jokes aside, this whole having-two-homes thing can be really tough and upsetting. You might feel confused and overwhelmed. But don't pull your hair out just yet! There are ways to make the situation easier. I have two words for you: get organized!

First, have a calendar that shows where you'll be every week of the year. This will help you plan ahead. As you get more used to your routines, you'll become a champion at swapping and switching, mixing and matching.

Second, make both your rooms feel comfortable. Work with your mom and your dad to make your rooms as fun and snug as you need them to be. You'll want to have a place where you feel safe, especially while you deal with the changes divorce brings. If one of your rooms is yucky, it will be very hard to spend time at that house—no matter how much you love that parent.

Let your parents know what is missing from one or both of your homes. It will be good to keep some basics, like clothes, toiletries, and school supplies at both homes. This is because you will forget things at one house when you go to the other. It's so easy to forget things when you're moving around.

Third, have a special "to-go" drawer at each house. Keep the things you travel back and forth with in the drawer. Make a habit of checking the drawer as you leave so you can just scoop up the stuff you need on the way out.

Going back and forth between two homes can be tough, especially if your parents live far apart. It's a good idea to keep in touch with the parent you see less often. A quick e-mail just to say "I'm thinking of you" can really help you—and them— feel better.

18
My parents are using me.

This is awful, but if the divorce is nasty, some parents forget that they need to protect their kids. They use them as message delivery systems, weapons against each other, or even spies.

If you find this happening, wait until your parents are not fighting with each other and then tell them how painful and upsetting their actions are. This might sound strange, but they may not even be aware of what their actions are doing to you.

If you find it hard to talk to them face-to-face, leave a phone message, e-mail them, or write them a letter. This will let them know what's on your mind, and putting things down on paper will also help you feel better.

Hey, I have an idea. If I make my parents feel guilty about getting divorced, then they'll feel sorry for me and give me stuff!

19
Gulp. I think I'm using my parents against each other.

This is a really difficult one, and you need to be honest with yourself. Sometimes young people who are going through a divorce realize that their parents are feeling guilty about the split-up, and they use this fact to get their parents to do things or buy them stuff they normally wouldn't. Some kids say one thing to one parent and something else to the other in order to play the parents against each other. This is called "manipulation," and it's not a nice thing to do.

Okay, I know that you might be angry and are saying things like, "Hey I need some lovin', man, and I'm going to do what it takes to get what I need. Like making my parents feel guilty."

This approach might work, but in the long run, being honest instead of playing games will be better for everybody. Rather than using your parents against each other, talk to them about your needs. You'll feel a lot better and you won't have to play games to get the love and care you deserve.

20
Things are getting broken and people are getting hurt.

If your parents become so angry that things get violent and stuff gets broken during fights, let them know how you feel immediately. You have a right to feel safe. If the behavior continues and you still feel unsafe, please tell someone you trust: a teacher, a grown-up you care about, your school counselor, your grandparents, or your priest or rabbi. It is not okay for you to be in danger during your parents' divorce, no matter how angry either of them may be.

21
Will holidays still be special?

Holidays might be hard to celebrate at first because they will be very different from holidays of the past. Try to accept the sad moments during holidays and cry about them if that makes you feel better. Over the years you will build new memories and traditions to enjoy and holidays will become easier to celebrate.

22
Okay, so what happens to me now?

I know things are changing and you don't like it, but unfortunately there is not much you can do except try to make the best of a tough situation. As your mom and dad go through their divorce, they will decide what's best for you. They will spend a lot of time figuring out when you will be with each of them.

They will also discuss the best way to take care of your needs. This is a very difficult time, and if you are worried about anything they are discussing, be sure to talk to one or both of them. Your concerns are important, and you need to let your parents know what's on your mind. Even though you might feel like a lost and forgotten sock inside a tumbling dryer, your parents love you and will take care of you.

23
Huh . . . so what do all these
divorce words mean?

Mostly your parents will take care of the legal stuff, so you won't have to worry about it. But you might hear some of these words during the divorce, and it'll be helpful to know what they mean. (I've also included some "unofficial" words that are just as important as the legal ones.)

Divorce: Legally ending a marriage.

Lawyer: A legal specialist who represents and advises parents during their divorce.

Judge: The "chief" in charge of the court. The judge decides how the divorce should be resolved.

Cry Buddy: A good friend or family member whose shoulder you can cry on when the divorce is getting too much for you.

Separation Agreement: A written document that describes the terms in which a marriage ends.

Custody: Custody refers to whom you will live with during and after the divorce. It might be with your mother, your father, or shared between them. In special circumstances grandparents, other relatives, or foster parents are given custody.

Humor Helper: Anything that makes you laugh during the divorce to help you cope. This includes funny movies, comics, and cartoons.

Child Support: The amount of money the parent who doesn't have custody will pay each month to help take care of you.

Alimony: Money one parent pays to support the other parent during or after the divorce.

Visitation: The time you will spend during or after the divorce with the parent who does not have custody.

24
Dating, oh gross!

Yikes! I'm about to mention something that might freak you out right now. Dating parents! Yep. Your divorced parents probably will start dating someone else at some time in the future. This might make you feel a little weird. It might even make you angry or sad. This is normal. Seeing your mom or dad with someone new will trigger some strange feelings.

You might not like your mother's new partner. You might compare him to your own dad. Or you might feel as if liking your dad's new partner is a betrayal of your mom. You might freak out because a parent dating makes it clear that your parents aren't going to get back together. You might fear that the new partner will take some of your parent's love away from you. All these feelings are perfectly understandable.

You need to remember that what your parents are doing is really just making new friends with other adults. Sometimes that friendship turns into romance. I know that sounds gross, but your parents aren't going to automatically marry the person they date. They are just trying to start new lives and have fun in the process, and that's good for them.

And don't worry. No new partner will steal the love your parents have for you. They might cause your parents to be a bit distracted for a while and act goofy or silly, but parents can be pretty silly and goofy anyway.

25
After all is said and done. . .

Right now you might still be in shock and you're sure not happy. But it won't always be this way.

As time goes by you will find it easier to accept your parents' divorce and the changes it brings. You may even discover some unexpected positives. Most kids discover their parents are actually happier after the divorce. They may even get along better with their parents when they have separate time with each one.

I know this might sound totally wacky, but coping with divorce can also bring out your strength and maturity. You might become more responsible, independent, and thoughtful. Some people become better problem solvers, better listeners, and even better friends.

Most kids discover—sometimes to their absolute amazement—that they can make it through this difficult situation successfully. Be patient. Let others support you and enjoy the good things in life. Be courageous. Be compassionate. Be creative. I wish you the absolute best as you go though this tough time. I have every faith that you will look back and say, "Whoa. That was tough, but dude, I did it. I took the 'duh' out of divorce."